A REP AGENCY'S ROAD MAP

TO DYNAMIC SALES PERFORMANCE

18 Hard-Hitting, Quick
Tips & Stories
To Explode Your
Sales & Profits

Charlie Hauck
Fred Liesong

A Rep Agency's Road MAP to Dynamic Sales Performance

A Growth Dynamics Book
Copyright © 2014, Growth Dynamics
All rights reserved.

No part of this book may be reproduced or transmitted in any form or by any means, electronic or mechanical, including photocopying, recording, or by any information retrieval system, without permission in writing from the publisher.

Book Cover by Tracey Miller | www.TraceOfStyle.com
Publishing by Weston Lyon | www.WestonLyon.com
Edited by Lauren Cullumber

ISBN: 1502329778
EAN-13: 978-1502329776

This book is not intended as legal, investment, accounting, or financial advice. The purchaser and/or reader of these materials assumes all responsibility for the use of this information. Growth Dynamics and Publisher assume no responsibility or liability whatsoever for any purchaser and/or reader of these materials. This book contains opinions, ideas, experiences, and exercises - and is not intended as financial advice. Please consult your financial and/or tax professional before adopting any of the suggestions in this book.

Dedication

The fact that this is not your typical book dedication will come as no surprise to the many rep agency clients we've worked with over the years. In fact, it is the trials, tribulations, commitment, and bravery of those very clients that have made this book possible.

So it only makes sense for us to dedicate this book to everyone who provided the true stories and inspiration for the real world content in each of the chapters.

Specifically, we wish to acknowledge the following:

- The amazing people who have applied our concepts to their own lives, and not just in the workplace.

- All the executives, managers and reps that had the guts to share their victories and nightmares in front of their peers.

- The company leadership teams that held our feet to the fire to make them better beyond their expectations.

- Those who willingly jumped into the program with both feet and made our made our work with them not just challenging, but enjoyable and thrilling at the same time.

- Those who came to understand that they could not control what was out of their control, and chose to work harder and smarter instead.

- Companies which acknowledged they were sincerely ready to grow, agreed to stop talking about it, and then made a plan with us to make it happen.

- Everyone who submitted to a self-assessment or profile and then accepted responsibility for learning about themselves.

Most importantly, we want to thank all of you for the questions you ask of everyone around you, the observations you make of yourself and others and the inspiration and energy you gave to the Growth Dynamics Team to write this book.

> *"Not everything that is faced can be changed, but nothing can be changed until it is faced."*
> **James Baldwin**

Table of Contents

Read This First 7

Section 1: Mindset 13

We're Still Friends, Aren't We? 15

Will Trumps Won't 17

Listen To The Voices Inside Your Head 19

How To Get On A Roll 23

Don't Be A Victim Of The Defection Model 25

Stick Up For Yourself 29

Section 2: Activity 31

Move It Or Kill It 33

Do You Major In the Minors? 35

Consistently Produce Stellar Results 39

How To Predict Future Sales And Income 43

Proper Planning Produces Pure Profits 47

Cold Calls Can't Compete With Referrals 49

Section 3: Process 51

Closing Is About Opening 53

Collecting Decisions To Close More Sales 55

The 3 Most Important Words! 59

Talking About Money 63

Can You Hear Me Now? 67

Can They Pass The Audition? 69

Final Thoughts **73**

Bonus Section **75**

Is Price Really The Issue? 77

Turn Desperation Into Courage 81

Miscommunication Is The Key To Failure 83

Bulldog Mentality Madness 87

Recipe For Success 89

Just Get Started Already 91

Get Out Of The Mind Reading Business 93

Are You Pushing Or Pulling? 95

About Charlie Hauck 99

About Fred Liesong 101

About Growth Dynamics 103

Hire Growth Dynamics To Speak 105

FREE Sales Performance Webcast 109

Read This First

This book is for Manufacturers Reps, Manufacturers, Wholesalers, Distributors and Contractors.

With that being said, we want to give you an opportunity to put this book right back down and not read another page. All of us at Growth Dynamics believe that you might be expecting to find something very different than what's in the pages that follow.

So consider this message a fair warning that you are not about to read a lot of feel-good stories about how great you already are or how wonderful it is to be in the world of sales.

Selling Is Hard.

At least selling at the highest levels of professionalism is hard, and in many cases considerably more difficult than some salespeople ever believed it could be when they entered this noble calling.

The challenge that many salespeople never fully face is that selling is a lot more than just being a people person, whatever that might mean, and knowing a lot about the features and benefits of your products or services. There is no doubt that some people are more gifted at sales than others. But there are very few that are so gifted that they don't have to work at improving the skills and truisms that the outside world believes some people acquire genetically.

There is no ivory tower theory anywhere in these pages. This book captures the real world experiences that our clients have shared with us over the years in their attempts to master the art of sales.

They have dared themselves to try something different, or to change their perception of what was really taking place when a salesperson and a prospect got together.

What we would like you to find in this book are a few examples of the scenarios or situations that frustrate you the most or leave you wondering what happened on a sales call.

For your convenience, we've broken this book into three sections that make up our MAP: MINDSET, ACTIVITY and PROCESS. Being proficient at each of these components is critical for sustained sales success.

Each section contains seven chapters. Each chapter begins with a summary, so you can quickly glance at each one and decide how it applies to your world. After each summary, we move into stories about how a client overcame the challenge and how you can, too.

No matter what level of sales you may be in, or how much experience you've accumulated in your career, we believe that the insights on each of these pages may provide you with enough of a different approach to be worth the relatively little time it would take you to read it from cover to cover.

Beyond that, we think it might be a good reference or place for you to search for an answer when a prospect seems more intent on how many hoops he or she can make you jump through than really doing business.

Over the years, we've had the benefit of working with thousands of salespeople, and that experience has taught us this simple truth: when the student is ready, the teacher will appear. So please give yourself the chance to let that come true for you and keep this little volume close by as you pursue sales success.

One more thing before you dive in looking for a magic bullet: over the years, the people who have proven to be our best students have always tended to be the ones that paid more than lip service to the phrase "room for improvement".

They knew it was about professional development and not about them as a person. In other words, their willingness to set aside ego driven personal emotions allowed them to become both coachable and trainable on the professional level.

What happened over the course of our time working with these folks is that they realized that to grow their business and to become more successful, what they were doing yesterday wasn't necessarily what was going to be the most productive and profitable for tomorrow.

So the choice is yours on whether or not you take this first step in following the lead of those who developed an open mindset.

Whether you are selling for an agency, running the firm, or perhaps doing both, what you are about to read will provide an opportunity to improve your sales performance and to experience more satisfaction, both personally and professionally.

Here's to exploding your sales and profits!

Charles P. Hauck

Fred H. Liesong

PS – We've included a Bonus Section for you on page 75. It includes 8 additional chapters to help you increase your sales. Enjoy!

PPS – We've also included information about a FREE Sales Performance Webcast for your team. You can read more on page 109.

PPPS - Here's what clients are saying...

"Our Sales Team is now better-equipped than ever. Our approach to market is now significantly more professional and effective. Every Agency owner and salesperson should pay attention to their message!"

Eric Lewis, President, Mullen Corp

"Charlie and Fred worked closely with our team to identify, and more importantly eliminate, the obstacles in the sales process. This caused us to really focus on what the true issues were, thereby transforming those real issues into new sales."

Paul Glum, President, PAMS Inc.

"We have used Charlie Hauck as our sales coach for 20 years. Several customers have asked us who we use as a trainer, so obviously they saw something from our sales team that stood out above the others."

Stew Chaffee, President, Rich-Tomkins Manufacturers Rep of the Year, 2014

"Finally, some information about selling that makes common sense. Liesong and Hauck give you a competitive advantage in performance that saves time and makes money!"

Russ Skog, CPMR, President, Brandon Associates

SECTION 1:
Mindset

Which came first, the chicken or the egg?

Does anyone really know? Does it really matter at this point? And what does this have to do with success in selling? The connection might be more important than you first realize when you talk about what it takes to raise your game to All-Star standards.

Which should come first, the mindset of success or success itself? For those that want to wait to be successful before thinking like you already are, the wait can often seem like an eternity. The winners are the professionals who understand that they must think the way a successful person would think and act the way a successful person would act before they can become successful. Whether you believe you can or cannot, you are definitely right!

Sales success happens as much between the ears and in the heart as it does between the salesperson and the prospect. It is more important to learn how to manage the internal messaging to support a positive outcome as it is to learn a great way to close or how to overcome stalls and objections. If the *courage* to use your selling tools is not present, the tools will not do you any good.

This chapter provides you with real world lessons on why "how you think" about sales success is much more important than "what you know" about features and benefits. Success is a choice, so read on and start enjoying the benefits of maintaining a MINDSET OF SUCCESS.

A Rep Agency's Road MAP to Dynamic Sales Performance

We're Still Friends, Aren't We?

"Friendship and Money: Oil and Water"
Mario Puzo

How often do business development professionals confuse friendship for business loyalty? Being more concerned about being liked than doing business, many salespeople make the fundamental mistake of allowing customers and clients to pay them with emotional currency and acceptance instead of continuing to give them orders. Emotional toughness is essential for avoiding this all-too-common sales killer.

Carl was feeling frustrated and hurt. One of his best accounts was showing a definite decline in volume that was way beyond what could be explained by the economy, and he could not imagine that he had done anything to create the change. Besides, the owner of the client company always said how much he enjoyed having Carl as a friend, someone he could count on when he needed something taken care of, or some "special" pricing. Carl felt good about this relationship and felt he could rely on it to keep him as the preferred supplier, no matter what. This situation made understanding why sales were heading south all the more frustrating.

Carl was guilty of one of the most common mistakes a salesperson can make: getting his emotional needs met on the job. By letting the relationship cloud his judgment, Carl probably missed a few hints about what was really happening at this account. Instead of recognizing signs of trouble, Carl was sure that the owner would certainly have told his good friend if there was anything amiss or if another vendor was aggressively pushing for the account. At worst, Carl would have a chance for the "last look" and was more than certain the friendship was worth a couple of dollars more than the competitor's low ball pricing.

The friendship stopped Carl from asking the tough questions, because he was totally dependent on the concept of "relationship selling." He was giving favors in the name of friendship and expecting the same in return, without having a clear understanding with his friend about the give and take.

Because we all want to be liked, Carl's situation can be hard to avoid. How many times have you heard someone claim that a client had taken advantage of the relationship, and when questioned about making a change heard the customer reply bluntly that "business is just business"?

Skilled sales professionals never forget that they are in sales to make money, not friends. That doesn't mean you cannot enjoy both benefits of the sales world, but confusing the two will lead to many disappointments and broken relationships.

In order to avoid the confusion that Carl felt, keep yourself from getting emotionally involved, and remember that your clients are business people first and friends second.

Will Trumps Won't

"If the word 'attitude' has become a cliché to you, then maybe it's time to evaluate your DESIRE, COMMITMENT, OUTLOOK AND RESPONSIBILITY."
Foundational Planks from Objective Management Group

Being highly successful in business development requires the commitment to do the things that average people believe can't be done. You never have to look far to find an acceptable excuse to go home early or not make that last call on a Friday afternoon. The will and commitment to being a consistent top performer will always produce better results than a performer who won't do the tough stuff that makes them uncomfortable.

Lauren hated reading the newspaper and watching the network news after work in the evening. It seemed like the "Big Story" everywhere was another report of a bankruptcy, people losing their jobs, a plane crash or other sad stories. The positive outlook Lauren typically brought to each day had always kept her going no matter what she encountered in her business development activities. But now, everyone she spoke with apparently felt like the good times would never return, and they all wanted her to join in their pity party. Looking at how hard she was working just to maintain some positive momentum, Lauren began to consider that those people might actually be right.

Anyone involved in business development will experience days that leave them feeling as if there is no hope and no reason to fight the fight, even when times are good. When the economy is stumbling along, the news sounds like no one is certain of anything anywhere. With some of her own relationships falling victim to the circumstances, Lauren's normal optimistic outlook could be expected to weaken. No one is immune to the noise and attitudes of others that have decided that failure is easier and that it's acceptable to give up. Her positive attitude was being challenged by the constant cry of those that had given up and wanted her to justify their decisions by joining them and giving up as well. If you hear something enough, you just might start believing it.

By reminding herself that her actions and her attitudes are the only two things she could totally control, Lauren was able to turn off the din of the news and those that had thrown in the towel. There was still a market out there that needed the services she was offering, and she figured if everyone else had given up then her opportunity had actually expanded. Survival of the fittest? When many decide that scarcity is an acceptable excuse, a few can benefit by seeing abundance. Lauren began each and every day repeating a mantra that was more powerful than the negative news, and consequently her activity increased, her focus became clearer and her decision-making became stronger. The words she chose were simple, but at the same time empowering: "My 'will' is always stronger than their 'won't'."

> Go to www.growdyn.com/map to learn more about the 4 Critical Elements of Success.

Listen To The Voices Inside Your Head

*"Falling down is how we grow.
Staying down is how we die."*
Brian Vaszily

No one hears any voice as clearly as they hear their own, and often the voice inside our head can be the loudest one of all. Self-talk that rings in our ears can determine success or failure in any endeavor. By learning how to program our internal messaging and to control the doubt and fear of negative self-talk, success becomes easier and less stressful to create.

Kathy was frustrated after a recent sales call. She believed that if she was brave enough to ask certain questions, the call should have gone her way. It seemed like she was constantly on defense and that the client was intentionally "pushing her buttons." Despite her training, it felt like she was always reacting to every little thing that was said rather than thinking about what was really going on. How can she find a way to consistently act like a professional on calls?

Amateur salespeople tend to get "emotionally" involved by overreacting to what buyers say during an interview. The emotions range from despair ("I'm losing this"), to anger ("I hate sales"), to excitement ("I own this guy"). Amateurs are too emotionally involved to function as a professional. They are frozen with emotion and miss opportunities to either turn a call around or close a deal.

Let's take a look at some winning ways:

- *"Nothing bad can happen during a conversation about business."*
~Charlie Hauck

- *"Things are never as good or bad as they seem at that moment."*
~John Condry

- *"It's not over, till it's over."*
~Yogi Berra

- *"I would be willing, yes glad, to see a battle every day during my life."*
~General George Armstrong Custer

- *"I will survive!"*
~Gloria Gaynor (Disco Reference!)

- *"You miss 100% of the shots you never take."*
~Wayne Gretzky

- *"You can't control others, only your response."*
~Unknown

- *"King Kong ain't got sh*t on me!"*
~Denzel Washington, "Training Day"

- *"I believe I will win."*
~Ken Jennings (Jeopardy champ!)

- *"What is the next step in my process?"*
~Professional with a Sales Process

Now, take these quotes – and your own favorites – and write each of them on a sticky note. Post them in your office, in your car, and at your home. And, make a commitment to reading them every time you see them for the next 30 days, so they become ingrained in your way of thinking.

How To Get On A Roll

"There are risks and costs to a program of action. But they are far less than the long-range risks and costs of comfortable inaction."
John F. Kennedy

Nothing beats the feeling of being on a roll, but nothing can be harder to figure out than how to get back in the groove when things aren't going the right way. Knowing the internal mechanisms and motivations of success can shorten the down cycles.

Matt was looking at his calendar and doing some planning, knowing that many things he does look too much like random acts of mindless behavior. Looking back on past months, he felt like he was scrambling and playing catch up all the time instead of having the feeling that he had deliberate control of his actions. He wanted to get that feeling of being on a roll, where it's like running downhill instead of uphill all the time.

Sure, the numbers speak for themselves, but he also understood that the numbers would come a lot easier if he had a mental plan that would give him some momentum. In the past he had been in a state of denial, which caused him to accept certain conditions and behaviors that mired him in mediocrity.

Matt developed a plan - he's going to focus on the big picture and avoid getting distracted by all the minor and non-productive diversions he may run into along the path. He knows that making a change will not happen overnight, and that he is going to have to go through smaller steps first if he wants to have a chance of turning things around.

In order to get on a roll, Matt is going to commit to the following sequence of thoughts and actions:

- Start with a vision, goal and plan based on principles and discipline in order to develop more control of his life.

- Expect to then become more self-assured, courageous, and action oriented in what he attempts.

- Anticipate success, and generate a pioneering spirit toward trying new things.

- Begin to realize steady growth in his personal and business life to the extent that **he *wants* to track his progress** so he can keep it moving in the right direction and catch any problems early.

- As these things happen, it generates a positive attitude and ***pride* in his accomplishments** along with *accepting responsibility* for whatever happens, good or bad.

- An abundance mentality begins to develop as he becomes aware there is plenty more out there he can do and accomplish.

All of these factors combine to increase Matt's self-confidence in his ability to produce a life of quality for himself and others.

Don't Be A Victim Of The Defection Model

"More business is lost every year through neglect than any other cause."
Rose F. Kennedy

The surprise of losing a longtime customer is one of the most painful things any salesperson can experience. The truth is, you rarely have any customer forever, but the sad part is that the defection could have been stopped before it happened in almost every case. Understanding the cycle of defection and the critical make or break moments are key to avoiding this painful experience.

Gary was having one of those days where he was angry, but also having some self-doubt. One of his biggest accounts had just informed him they were switching to another vendor. All of this came as a great surprise, and he knew these events would create a whirlwind of damage control, finger pointing, and endless postmortems. His first thought was that they were just jerks, but something was nagging at him about how this could have happened on his watch.

When this happens, all too often the situation is well past the point of no return. The defectors have worked their way through the exit process right in front of us without our even seeing it. The response is often to point the finger at anyone but ourselves and write it off as evidence that there just isn't any loyalty anymore. Gary just wasn't willing to admit that he and his team ignored all the signals and let complacency dictate their approach. His false expectation was that if someone was thinking about leaving, then they would speak up on their own.

The Defection Model has a definitive progression:

Step 1: An event is the catalyst that starts the defection model in motion:

- Lack of response to a problem or complaint
- Competition knocking at their door
- A cross word, a style conflict or a problem with perceived tone
- Indifferent attitudes
- Poorly planned meetings

Step 2: Introspection:

- Is this just the tip of the iceberg?
- Why is there a struggle about almost everything?
- Maybe I should be looking at other options.
- My agenda always seems less important than theirs.
- I deserve more respect than this.

Step 3: Due Diligence. It's time to do their homework, so they:

- Request copies of contracts and agreements and other documentation to prepare their case

- Start making unreasonable requests (looking for a reason to quit)
- Stall on any activity that implies a renewed commitment
- Don't return phone calls or emails
- Seriously consider the alternatives and the competition

Step 4: Deciding to defect:

- Keep it on the "QT"
- Plan their exit strategy
- Prepare to SPIN their reasons for leaving
- Build their case against you
- Make the Announcement
- Make it Official

If you are alert and take proactive action in step one and two, your chances of saving the situation are better. However, once they move to step three, your success rate drops considerably. And, at step four, it will take a miracle or a huge concession to get them back.

A Rep Agency's Road MAP to Dynamic Sales Performance

Stick Up For Yourself

"Nobody can make you feel inferior without your consent."
Eleanor Roosevelt

Business professionals who allow themselves to be victimized will have a less than satisfying career. Even salespeople have rights, but few will take the time to learn what they are and how to protect themselves through actively taking responsibility. Wanting or expecting customers and prospects to treat you any differently than other vendors is only a matter of how you allow them to treat you.

Jim was feeling discouraged and wasn't sure how he could make it through another week like the one before. A new prospect had made him wait over 30 minutes before he would see him, and then asked Jim to sell to him at his cost. Another client had told him he was backing out of a deal they had made just two days before, and that it was none of his business how that happened. This wasn't the first time that people had treated him this way and he was beginning to wonder just how much he had to grovel before he could do business with folks like this.

Admittedly, the business world can be cruel at times, and you can't expect to be treated like royalty or get everything you want all the time. Getting your emotional needs met on the job is usually a low percentage play...so quit trying. Perhaps your energy is better spent on understanding your rights in a business transaction and then sticking to them without any arrogance.

Many clients understand the ethics and etiquette of the business world, but there are others that will take advantage of you if you don't have a firm understanding of how you should be treated. It doesn't matter if you've been in sales for years or you're just getting started - what matters most is that you don't get treated like someone on a different caste level.

Salespeople have rights just like anyone else:

- I have a right to know where I stand with a customer or prospect. (Don't forget to ask!)

- I have a right to find out why I'm not getting a particular contract.

- I have a right to say "No" to a bad deal and walk away.

- I have a right to be treated with respect.

- I have a right to ask questions, of anyone, so that I can understand more clearly and perform more effectively.

- I have a right to like and approve of myself...even if others at times may not.

- I have a right to help my company grow profitably and to advance my career and income in doing so.

- I have a right to exercise my rights at all times.

You probably have more of your own to add, so just remember that your firm provides goods and services for profit and that you are essential to your clients.

SECTION 2:
Activity

Cold calls, referrals, closing ratios, openings, decision meetings, dials, pipeline, sales cycle: these are the words of sales activity. No matter what labels you put on the steps of your process, or how you calculate the math of your success, there is one truth that never can be denied: Sales is a game of numbers. The variable is you and how you generate those numbers.

Success in selling requires accountability for activity. And whether anyone likes it or not, all of the numbers are interconnected and must be analyzed collectively for true accountability. High closing percentages do not indicate sales success if you don't generate enough opportunities to hit your quota or target. On the other hand, many salespeople are really active but never convert that activity into productivity. Understanding the diagnostic value of activity accountability is essential for sales teams as well as individuals.

Too often our experience in sales success mimics the behavior of a college student that cuts class all semester and tries to cram for the final exam to get a passing grade. It may work once in a while, but over the long term that practice becomes unreliable.

Sales success requires consistency of activity through all the steps of your sales process. Very few people succeed in sales trying to make their numbers at the end of every month. This chapter contains scenarios that deal with the importance of maintaining consistent activity and understanding the importance of being accountable for that activity.

Move It Or Kill It

"Indecision and delays are the parents of failure."
George Canning

"Man, my pipeline is full," can mean two things. Someone is really prospecting or someone has not actually advanced all the opportunities he or she has accumulated. A full pipeline that has a lot of old and dusty cases is a pipeline that needs attention. Salespeople must learn to move things through the pipeline to a decision. Are you one of those people that understands you have to move it or kill it?

Alice was at her wit's end. After three months of hard work, moving step by step towards the final decision, the sales process was stuck. She had worked the system well, but had failed to get either a Yes or a No answer while she was in front of the client. Now her calls were not being returned by the client. Alice had put too much work into the account to walk away, and she was smart enough to know that the selling isn't over until she said it's over. However, she was uncertain how to proceed if she couldn't find out what was going on behind the scenes at the account.

She wanted to get movement one way or another so she could get the information she needed to decide how to proceed. With proper knowledge, she would be able to make the decision to move it or kill it on her own terms.

In retrospect, Alice realized she wasn't persistent enough during the last call to find out if there was a "No" there somewhere, and now she has lingering doubts about whether she even had a deal in the first place. She would know the answer by now if she had taken the time to schedule a decision meeting or put a deadline on the end of the process.

There are a number of options to get the process moving:

- Offer to "fire" yourself for not getting this deal off their desk.

- Ask the account if you have misread the earlier signals that you were going forward.

- Write off the account and move on. Time kills deals and this one might have already been dead.

- If it's important enough, then do "whatever it takes" to move it or kill it.

- Give them the pen and ask what the deal would look like so that when they agree, they know they made a good decision.

In a competitive environment, the sale isn't over until it's over. Sometimes they decide, sometimes you do. **Taking action steps removes the pressure and eliminates the agony of how to proceed.** With a full pipeline, Alice can deal with this account from a position of strength.

A Rep Agency's Road MAP to Dynamic Sales Performance

Do You Major In the Minors?

"Some folks can look so busy doing nothing that they seem indispensable."
Kin Hubbard

Everyone likes to appear busy as much as possible. It tends to justify our existence, but frequently it's not enough to be busy without true results. How many people do you know that are so busy and self-important that they are usually "running late," show up unprepared, frequently miss deadlines and have trouble driving enough of the right things to completion?

Jody was driving away from her newly won account with that smirky smile of satisfaction on her face. She had walked her way through the process from the referral stage, onto discovery and fact finding, then qualification with a commitment to act one way or another, and finally the agreement to do business together.

She knew her self-satisfaction was a result of the actions she took only a few short weeks ago, after several nightmare appointments almost sent her to rock bottom. During those calls, she had been nervous about her lack of preparation and from not knowing where she was in her own sales cycle. All that should have been done did not get done because she kept telling herself she was "too busy" to spend the needed time on any one aspect of her business.

Different people have different styles when it comes to managing the activities needed to be successful in the business world. Jody was not one of those that was very good at "winging it," and felt much more confident when she had her ducks lined up. When she was forced to "wing it," the lack of control she felt easily derailed her process. Even though she understood this about herself, it seemed like there was always another phone call, another person asking for her help or some seemingly easy task that turned into a major project. This tendency to try and tackle everything had led to a messy calendar, a chaotic and nervous thought process, and a flurry of frenetic activity that caused even more stress and anxiety.

Jody's recent string of successes was a result of her determination to regain control of her weekly activities. Even the best tools and methods for setting priorities or "time management" are useless if they don't get used consistently. Too often we find ourselves driving the car while looking at the hood ornament and then run head-on into the big huge obstacle only a mile down the road.

To prevent yourself from majoring in the minor things, try these tips:

- Be brutally honest with yourself about how and where you spend your time. Business planning is important, but so is personal time.

- Learn how to say "NO" in a nurturing manner. It's very difficult to keep everyone happy all the time.

- Plan for contingencies. In a complex world, things are often not as easy or simple as they seem.

- Delegate when possible. You can't control everything, so sometimes you just have to let it go.

- Resist taking on too many tasks or activities that aren't directly related to the achievement of your goals.

Sure, tomorrow is important, but so are next week and next month. Take the time to see the big picture and you'll find yourself getting out of "pinball" mode. Pick a system that works for you and that isn't so complex that it becomes a time waster itself.

A Rep Agency's Road MAP to Dynamic Sales Performance

Consistently Produce Stellar Results

"If you're not consistently carrying out your plan ninety percent of the time, you really don't have a plan at all."
Alwyn Cosgrove

Too many salespeople train themselves to ride the highs and lows of inconsistent production. One month the results are outstanding, but then the next two months are spent rebuilding and waiting for another month to be magic again. How would your organization be impacted if your sales team could produce consistently high numbers month after month, instead of asking for permission to stay on the roller coaster for another ride?

Mike had just received his sales results for the previous month, and the report showed that his production had started to drop off. After a very quick start, Mike had no doubt that the year was a lock and that he only needed to stay on a roll to finish at the top of the heap. Driving home from the office, he reviewed how his year had been going and looked for ways to make sense of his inconsistent production. Mike had no trouble coming up with all the reasons (or were they really excuses?) that he believed justified the downward spiral from his quick start at the beginning of the year. What happened to his momentum?

Mike's plight occurs in the sales world as commonly as head colds in the winter. This up-and-down stuff is often accepted by many sales people and managers as a part of the sales game. It's all too easy to repeat the familiar excuses: too many service calls, too busy with paperwork to make calls, no one would call him back, new products take time to gain traction, tech support or customer service dropped the ball, and many others that seem acceptable, yet obviously do not contribute to the top line.

The problem is that the real reasons are right in front of him, *but he lacks a system to understand how he really spends his time without doing a lot of mental gymnastics.* Working without a plan, failure to make a commitment to better activity levels, being more worried about closing a particular sale than opening enough opportunities, and other "non-pay time" activities that get in the way of doing the tough stuff are self-inflicted barriers that are rooted in self denial. He is not stupid, or lazy, and although he wants to believe he is doing all the right stuff, *he knows that he must find a better way to track how much time he is really spending on highly productive activities.*

Successful sales professionals that consistently produce stellar results generally have some common traits that separate them from the middle of the pack performers. By developing a commitment to do the things the pros do every day, Mike will find himself leaving his days of inconsistent results behind.

First, the elite performers know nothing will happen unless they create a plan for achieving the goals they set. These best of the best understand that more than anything, creating enough opportunities has the greatest impact on how easily they achieve their goals. If there are not enough opportunities in the top of the funnel, you can never expect to get enough out of the bottom. **With that in mind, each week is committed to doing the behaviors that appear on the 100 points per week list.** Now he has a way to track all the really valuable efforts, such as joint sales calls, scheduling decision meetings, placing new product displays, and utilizing a variety of sales approaches (prospecting) as needed to fill the pipeline and keep it in motion.

Lastly, the real consistent winners take responsibility for what happens to them. The practice of doing what others will not, or cannot, commit to do is normal to this group at the top. Hearing a "No" is as valuable as getting a "Yes" to the pros because they understand the difference between the person and the performance, and truly care about doing whatever it takes to improve their performance.

> Visit our Resource Center at www.growdyn.com/map to download a generic template for the 100 Point Week.

A Rep Agency's Road MAP to Dynamic Sales Performance

How To Predict Future Sales And Income

"The Pipeline, if managed properly with the right tools, should be the single most accurate predictor of future sales revenue. Do you have gold bullions or lumps of coal in yours?"
Dave Kurlan

Salespeople hate pipelines, or at least most of them do, because they don't understand how a pipeline is really meant to be utilized. A well-managed pipeline is fluid, meaning that an opportunity that enters the pipeline can be managed to a decision instead of just being entered and hoping that something will happen next. Pipelines are meant to tell you the future, not the past. Of utmost importance, good managers recognize the significant value of pipelines as a great coaching tool and should never ever be used as a weapon of mass destruction.

Marv is a good prospector and finds it easy to keep his pipeline very full. He prospects regularly and prides himself on a pipeline that most people could only dream of creating. His personality and persistence give him the chance to spend lots of time with potential customers that do not mind spending time either face to face or on the phone with Marv. Despite this seemingly ideal selling condition, Marv's recent meeting with his sales manager revealed that his pipeline appeared impressive because of its size, but in reality was just a bloated, stagnant list of the same old names. How could that be?

Marv suffers from a disease many sales people find at the root of their frustration, as well as the management's. Relying on his strength as a prospector keeps Marv with a full funnel, but he has not mastered the art of bringing those opportunities to a conclusion. His pipeline just continues to grow and grow to the point where he can't possibly do all the "follow up" work he loves to do and that doesn't result in enough orders.

His emotional side is getting in the way of creating urgency, and he has a deep-seated belief that he will close almost every opportunity that is out there if he can just keep them on the line long enough. Without a commitment to look at why he does not advance the process, and is not willing to stop chasing people, Marv may never figure out why all of his expended energy still does not produce the outcomes he really desires. He is definitely working hard and has a lot of persistence, but he is confused about how to convert his massive pipeline into commissions.

Marv and his sales manager need to develop a process that allows both of them to discern the patterns that keep him in this vicious cycle. Until some methods are implemented to see where he turns into a chaser, as opposed to becoming a closer, there is little hope of providing coaching or effective training to overcome this situation.

Marv may suffer from a consistent need to be liked, a fear of failure, lack of an "abundance mentality" or a fear of hearing "No." Perhaps he just isn't strong enough to suggest that there might not be a good fit to see if the prospect will defend their status as a potential client. The strength of Marv's persistence may have compromised his commitment to be a strong decision maker, or eroded a willingness to hear "Yes or No" in a time frame that meets his manager's expectations. Until he commits to changing his beliefs about what make his efforts truly effective, there can be little reason to expect the success to follow the effort.

Proper Planning Produces Pure Profits

"If you don't control your time, then somebody or something else will. The only thing you can do to control time is deciding what to do with it."
Growth Dynamics Voodoo

Time is really never an event. Time is a measurement of duration. Salespeople need to know how to set the expectations for the duration of a decision process. If you ask when they expect to get an answer, most salespeople will tell you it takes as long as it takes. Good selling doesn't exist with random expectations, but instead, uses time expectations as a way to manage the success ratios and sales strategies.

Jake was putting in about 60 hours a week plus some time on the weekends, but was still worried that his sales and management production was not nearly as high as it could be. The family didn't see him as much anymore and his "To Do" list was constantly growing. Despite all his hard work, the only thing he could conclude was that he needed to do a better job of "time management."

Jake's conclusion is partly right, but he might be working on the wrong end of the problem. Instead of managing his time, he may want to start managing himself.

His days had become disjointed with dozens of different activities and distractions. He was spending several hours with his reps on four days out of five, answering the phone every time it rang, constantly watching his email, taking a sales appointment whenever he could get one, doing paperwork in between, and trying to sneak in some time for prospecting when he wasn't being interrupted with everything else.

It's not unusual for many reps and managers to have the same problem when trying to manage dozens of different, unrelated tasks and still get some time off. One of the best ways to work around this is to schedule similar activities in blocks well BEFORE someone else (or something else) finds a way to eat up your day.

Jake decided to schedule certain blocks or days on his calendar for three distinct types of activities - some for production, some for planning and admin work, and some for recovery and personal time. Now he already knows in advance which days he can fill with sales appointments, which days or blocks he will stay in the office to prospect, which time slots are for management, and which days he will leave open for personal time. By pre-scheduling openings for similar activities, he can actually get something done and get on a roll with whatever he has decided to do with that particular block of time. If he can stay loyal to his calendar, and jealously guard what he has planned for himself, then he will find that his days are much less fractured and much more productive.

A Rep Agency's Road MAP to Dynamic Sales Performance

Cold Calls Can't Compete With Referrals

"Prospecting is like buying life insurance; nobody likes doing it, but everyone is glad they did when the payoff arrives."
Charlie Hauck

Cold calls are the badge of honor for many an old sales dog. The toughness and commitment it takes to make cold calls is one of the fundamental success factors in selling. If you have nothing left to do, cold calls are a great use of time, but there are very few things in selling that are as inefficient and ineffective as cold call-based sales.

Surviving another day of cold calling was almost more than Maria could bear. Day after day, she had been doing what all the books she'd read about sales told her was the real key to long term success. That meant dialing another couple dozen numbers, despite the dread and demoralizing effect it was having on her will to survive. Sure, the calls she made during her first six months of "new person probation" had yielded her some nice accounts, but was cold calling really getting her where she wanted to be?

Many old-school sales managers want Maria right where she is: working like a dog doing low percentage cold calling. She needed a way to create more high quality new accounts with fewer initial contacts, thus allowing her to maintain her high standard of service and seeing her client list grow as her numbers improved. It had become abundantly clear to her that more of the same diet of cold calls was not going to get her where she wanted to go.

Cold calls are a good way to build a strong sales process foundation for anyone, and some cold calling is usually necessary. But pound for pound, cold calls are also the least efficient way to get more business in terms of time and energy. Maria was forced to find out how to train her existing accounts and relationships to become part of her sales team. Enlisting those people to provide a steady stream of referrals and introductions will provide better-qualified first contacts and much shorter sales cycles.

With this process, she could now invest even more time with the best accounts, building stronger, more profitable relationships that would in turn provide her with even more referrals and introductions. The first thing all real sales pros should learn after establishing a strong base of business is how to mine that base for more of the same types of customers. Once Maria learned this invaluable skill, she found herself with more time and a growing list of "A" and "B" clients.

SECTION 3:
Process

How often have we heard a battle-hardened sales guy explain his success by saying, "I don't know how I do it, but whatever I do seems to work." That lack of understanding creates a number of problems for both the individual and the sales team.

For the sales guy, the lack of awareness of his tactical maneuvers will leave him floundering and frustrated when that behavior doesn't work consistently. How can he fix something when he cannot honestly identify what might be broken in the first place? The team suffers when eager young people have to be mentored or trained by the more senior team member that cannot identify what really works or what really doesn't.

Sales should never be a game that is played on automatic pilot. True professionals develop skills and processes that allow them to operate efficiently and effectively on a sales call, but just as importantly allow them to debrief the experience for their own benefit or for the benefit of teaching and developing others. Using a consistent process and knowing where you are in that process will allow you to manage yourself to success, and to truly get out of the world of "dog and pony shows" and "show up and throw up" selling.

This chapter includes tactics and process management tools that you may be familiar with. However, what we have found over the years is that far too many salespeople don't know how, when, or why they should utilize these tools. Our goal is for you to develop the awareness, as well as the tactical proficiency, that a strong sales process can provide.

Closing Is About Opening

"The top of the funnel is like oxygen to sales production. Without oxygen, breathing becomes difficult. Without relief, difficult breathing can often become suffocation."
Charlie Hauck

With all the attention placed on closing percentages and closing deals there should be little surprise that salespeople primarily focus on that end of an opportunity. That very same attention creates the pressure that causes most prospects to dislike being sold. Sales success really comes from *opening* an opportunity correctly and allowing the close to happen naturally and comfortably for both the salesperson and the prospect.

Mike looked at his monthly sales report and did not like what he saw. Despite working harder than he had all year, the numbers told Mike that he could forget about getting his quarterly bonus. It seemed like each quarter turned out the same; one month that Mike thought would carry him to a bonus and two months that fell short. The pattern was frustrating for Mike as he tried to figure a way to break into the top performer group in his office. It seemed like all the wins he posted in the one good month stole the time he needed to prospect for the other two months. Besides, how could anyone be expected to stop the customer service fire drills that popped up all the time? Mike was beginning to feel trapped.

Many salespeople struggle to find the balance between prospecting, closing opportunities and servicing existing business. Mike's results typified those struggles, and unless he could understand the behavior patterns that kept repeating, things were not bound to change. The one thing that will never change is the amount of time available to us to get everything done... 24 hours a day will always be 24 hours a day, no matter how much we wish it would change. Mike had the same amount of time to produce the results that the real top performers had to work with each day. What Mike struggled with was consistency of effort, and committing to doing the right things, no matter what else came up.

Sales success starts with prospecting or marketing and the most successful salespeople commit to that task every day, week in and week out. By making sure that you know how many calls you need to make each week, and not letting anything get in the way of meeting that goal, you give yourself the best chance of becoming a true sales leader. The ups and downs that salespeople live with will flatten out and turn into consistent performance if you stay focused on the right activity behaviors.

Create a success formula for the amount of prospecting needed to meet your goals, track the length of your sales cycle and track your performance against those standards. Only then will you see if you are doing the most fundamental thing that will lead to consistent sales success and end the monthly or quarterly stress of making your numbers.

Remember, there is nothing to close if you don't open something!

Collecting Decisions To Close More Sales

"Never agree to anything unless you know what is supposed to happen next."
Charlie Hauck

When did it become the common belief that YES was the only valuable and possibly allowable outcome in a sales conversation? True sales professionals know their numbers, including how many yes and no decisions they can expect to collect. The only thing worse than getting a "No" is not getting any answer at all, and then being forced to let an opportunity die on the vine without a final decision. A salesperson's real job is not to get a "Yes" at every opportunity, but to get a *decision* at every opportunity.

Pete was facing the usual challenge that most salespeople face every day. How would he know when to try to "close" the sale? He had heard that a salesperson's job is not to close, but to help buyers get off the "think it over" fence.

Closing starts by working with qualified opportunities that are willing to make a decision. Most salespeople can't wait to make a presentation in front of anyone that will listen, because they don't have much traction to begin with anyways. When a poor job has been done qualifying, we find that presentations are not very effective and cause a high "think it over" rate. When salespeople do not set up **decision expectations**, buyers feel no accountability to the process. *When* *this happens, any efforts at business development are really just professional visiting.*

Now fast forward to your presentation. Let's pretend you had to give a presentation right now to a buyer who you had not spoken with about the expectations of getting to either a Yes or a No in some agreed upon time frame. You don't know their process, who has authority, or if there's anything in their world you can help them solve. So you press on. You'd have to tell them about every problem, need, and want that your product or service addresses, wouldn't you? You couldn't leave anything out. You'd lead with your most important features and continue right down to your least important. You'd discuss each feature, its benefits and how it solves the problem.

Since the buyer has not been given a chance to tell you what he is looking for, or even if he is willing to move the process forward, he is under no obligation to respond to your presentation or proposal with a decision. *Buyers rarely feel any guilt when you give them all your information and they give nothing in return.*

> Visit our Resource Center at www.growdyn.com/map for a Description of "Buyers School" and the common traps that lead to a confused sales cycle.

Let buyers know early in the process that you will give them a presentation or a proposal in exchange for a decision. Never leave a meeting without an agreement to do something that moves the deal toward a decision of Yes or No. At the very least, never leave a meeting without scheduling the next. Try to remember B.A.M. – Book Another Meeting. Little commitments throughout the sales process lead to big results on the sales board. With every "Sale of the Moment," you will move that much closer to a decision.

The 3 Most Important Words!

"The three best closing words in sales ... 'Are you sure?'"
Charlie Hauck

Closed at the meeting and lost on the drive back to the office! This phrase rings true for many salespeople who can't muster the courage to ask this three-word question: *Are You Sure?* Too often the excitement of the yes overwhelms a hungry salesperson to the point that he can't even begin to imagine the sale could still be in jeopardy. If there are any surprise disappointments lurking out there, then make them happen when you're face-to-face instead of getting a voicemail or an email with the bad news. Learn to never close twice.

After a long sales process finally appeared to be coming to a successful conclusion, Paul was breathing a sigh of relief until his client decided he wanted to extract some sweat from Paul for the win. Just when he thought it was over and done, the regional vice president chimed in with one last contract change that he claimed was a deal breaker if it wasn't accommodated. Once the shock and anger had subsided, Paul collected his thoughts and recalled his training that brought this exact situation up in a role-play scenario. "Fool me once, shame on you. Fool me twice, shame on me" was the phrase echoing through his brain, as Paul was sure not to be the fool another time.

Last minute deal breakers have been a favorite tactic of prospects since the beginning of sales history. Buyers like to take advantage of an emotionally charged salesperson that is so close to cashing in that they sometimes relish the thrill of throwing a last minute curveball into play. These eleventh hour demands can be critical points for closing a deal, so they should never be taken lightly. But they can also be the last play in a battle that turns a good deal into just another expensive sale that has to be delivered at a lower price. Paul was standing right there and was sharp enough to realize it.

Getting his emotions back under control was the first, best thing Paul did after getting the surprise request. Once he had regained his equilibrium, Paul could start to protect the good work he had already done up to that point. Rather than arguing about what a good deal he had already given them, Paul asked the critical questions that would determine the real truth about the prospect's intentions. First he discovered if the demand was a make or break reality with a "If we can't meet this request, does that mean it's over and it will never ever happen?"

With the conversation back open again and the answer now on the table, he knew now what would happen if he didn't agree. So Paul now had to work to make sure that he only had to close this again one time and one time only. Before taking the change back to his manager for a final blessing, Paul had to be assured that this was the real last condition to be met. So pulling from his training, he asked firmly, but politely, "If I get this taken care of, what happens next?" When the prospect answered in a manner that assured him of his sale, Paul did a final gut check and asked the words he often regretted not getting out of his mouth before: "Are you sure?" With an extended hand and a confident nod, the client replied, "Yes, now can you go get this order placed, please?"

Talking About Money

"Winners are not afraid of losing. But losers are. Failure is part of the process of success. People who avoid failure also avoid success."
Robert T. Kiyosaki

Unless you're working for a charity and you don't have to get paid for your product or your service, the topic of money *must* be dealt with in every sales opportunity. Culturally, many people nowadays have been taught that talking about money (especially when it isn't yours) is impolite and should be avoided. All the features and benefits in the world won't make a prospect that has no money very comfortable with that subject. Dealing with money at the right time, all the time, protects everybody in the conversation.

Matt was leaving his last sales call with the belief that he had been beaten again because of his price. Knowing that he was not the lowest price on the block, he had given the purchasing agent prospect his best consulting expertise up front in an attempt to build his "value proposition" and then tried to save the money discussion for the end so as not to scare them away too early. He willingly even offered a 10% discount as soon as they mentioned that his price was higher than what they were currently paying to the guy down the street. Thinking he had done everything he could, there was no choice other than to go back to the office and tell his manager they had lost yet another deal because their prices were too high.

Matt had a belief about money that came from his own personal money struggles and buying habits that made him nervous and uneasy when talking about money or his prices. It hadn't occurred to him that not all his clients were buying every product or service at the lowest price available, and that some would be willing to pay a little more if it will make their pain and problems go away. He had allowed himself to be victimized by the professional buying skills of a purchasing agent that did not have the real picture about the investment versus the goals, and had therefore made a pre-judgment that he would never get the deal without beating the existing price or giving away his margin and expertise. His inability to withstand the money pressure had been compromised by not having any clear picture about why they were even talking in the first place.

A low-grade fever caused by money discomfort can often be cured with a few mental and strategic treatments:

• Talk about the tough stuff earlier rather than later. Ask them to help you talk about price, timelines or budget issues.

• Remember that certain players might only know how much they won't spend, and don't know how much they will spend. Are you talking to the right people?

• If you are worried about not being the lowest, then tell them that up front when discussing expectations.

• Understand the difference between your money and their money. You aren't paying their invoices.

- Develop a strong understanding of your own money matters so that it doesn't cloud your selling process.

- Talk in "round numbers" or "off the record" to get money issues on the table.

A Rep Agency's Road MAP to Dynamic Sales Performance

Can You Hear Me Now?

"It was impossible to get a conversation going because everybody was talking too much."
Yogi Berra

Just because you said it to a buyer or customer does not mean they heard it. Active listening and effective communicating are skills that must be developed and constantly employed to reach the highest levels of business success. Too many salespeople become so consumed by their ability to present a product or a value proposition that they turn off their ability to pick up and process the communication from the other side of the transaction. Business conversations require equal commitment and participation from both the buyer and the seller, but it is the seller's job to make that happen.

Cliff was surprised. He told the customer how things would work out, and when the customer disagreed he told him again. And again, and again. Then his manager got an angry phone call asking that he not be sent back, because the client didn't see any way for Cliff to handle their account. Cliff was indignant. Didn't the client understand that Cliff was the expert and knew best what the client really wanted?

Cliff needs to become an Active Listener. An active listener does just that. He listens and tries to see the prospect's point of view, paying attention not only to the words spoken, but to the thoughts and ideas behind the content. Cliff is always too busy trying to figure out which part of his pitch he is going to deliver next. His ego takes over and the only thing on his agenda is making sure the client understands that he has the only right answer. Without the proper questions, Cliff can only keep talking instead of listening.

Here are some tips on how to become an Active Listener:

- Concentrate by focusing your attention on your contact and only your contact.

- Acknowledge the person by demonstrating your interest and attention. Use cushions like "makes sense" and "glad you asked that" but do NOT be overly redundant with those questions to the point where it becomes boring and predictable.

- Ask good, direct pointed questions to gather information about the situation.

- Sense the non-verbal messages they are sending out. Be part of the moment and not a reactionary.

- Ask if it's OK to take notes to show you are interested.

Active Listeners listen *behind* the words for the thoughts and feelings, and listen *between* the words for what is not being said aloud.

Sometimes prospects reveal more by what they don't say than what they do say. There are several ways to determine the emotions behind the words. Eye contact, body language, pitch and tone are just a few examples. The only way to listen is to quit talking.

A Rep Agency's Road MAP to Dynamic Sales Performance

Can They Pass The Audition?

"Don't go around saying the world owes you a living. The world owes you nothing. It was here first."
Mark Twain

No one gets a part in the production until they pass the audition. Just because someone has interest in what you're selling doesn't qualify them for the role of a true prospect. Unless they pass the audition, meaning they have qualified for the part of prospect, a suspect will remain just that and should be treated appropriately. The best reps understand the critical difference between those that are simply "interested" and those that are really willing to make a commitment to the buying and selling process.

Brian had just made a proposal to a buyer and received the same response he has heard so many times recently. "Thanks for the proposal. Appreciate you coming in. We'll give it some consideration and let you know." The buyer seemed unimpressed by the entire conversation, and our sales pro knew that the chances of getting any business were slim and none. Late-breaking news flash: "Slim" had just left the building.

Salespeople continually spend far too much time with prospects that are unworthy of their time and presentation. The warning signs are there, but they are ignored. They stay with their losing hand, hoping to catch an improbable card on the river. This happens primarily because salespeople typically have weak pipelines and are desperate to meet with anybody. Their primary strategies are to grind them down or hope to get "lucky."

Brian needs to be able to audition each contact quicker to determine their worthiness to see his "magic dust." Your time is valuable, and prospects will think nothing about wasting it. They want your information and don't care about the agony they might be putting you through with their antics.

So before you decide to invest any serious time with a buyer, make them pass a worthiness interview. If you can honestly answer yes to the following questions, then they most definitely have earned the right to your time. If not, find a different product, a different approach, or find a better prospect.

- Are they willing to talk about their business?
- Will they allow you to ask about pain, problems, and priorities?
- Do they know what they want?
- Do they want it in a reasonable time frame?
- Assuming you "wow" them, can they make an investment?

All buyers need to earn your continued involvement with them. It's not a one-way street. If they don't pass the test, explain to them (without a hint of arrogance or frustration) that you probably don't have a good fit. This tactic can get their attention real fast and can help them to disqualify themselves. Their hesitancy to share information and/or their inability to articulate what they really want lets you know that this is just another trip on the Crazy Train to Nowhere for both of you.

Don't hang in there hoping that they will turn into a great prospect, because they probably won't. Disengage and move on to someone who is a more worthy candidate or to a different product area that has better potential. There are plenty of good opportunities out there if you'll ramp up your new business development efforts.

Final Thoughts

Did you hear, see, feel, or learn something new? Did you find even one simple nugget you can or will use in your everyday efforts?

If so, congratulations on being open minded enough to let some new concepts inside your world. If you found more than one concept you are committed to using, then maybe you are starting to build something that really sings. That song could be a wonderful thing in the business world, where excuses, stalls, entitlement, defeatism, and unproductive behavior can start to sound like the deafening and irritating noise of a gaggle of geese. For being determined to block out that noise, go ahead and give yourself a pat on the back for the bravery to elevate your game.

On the other hand, if you found nothing you can use and thought it was all hogwash, then that's OK too. We know these ideas are not for everyone. We understand that embracing change and letting go of traditional beliefs may undermine a personal success formula you are already using. Sincerely, we do. So no matter what your circumstances, please be aware that we gladly welcome your feedback and would love hearing from you.

Thanks for reading this book, or at least some of the stories. We hope you learned some interesting and exciting concepts that you can use to make yourself different in such a competitive environment. We see so many companies and individuals try to differentiate themselves through pushing features, benefits, pricing, or programs and forget about this one single idea...**perhaps the best way to stand out from the crowd is to get someone's attention *by the questions you ask, the way you think, how you position yourself and the fact that your approach is not what they see or expect from everyone else.***

So we'll leave you with this last question...

If you act and behave like a typical vendor, do you have any reason NOT to be treated like every other vendor?

Here's to exploding your sales and profits!

Charles P. Hauck

Fred H. Liesong

PS – We thought you'd enjoy some bonus material, so see the next page for 5 additional lessons to help you sell more, faster.

PPS – If you have enjoyed the concepts in this book, then you're going to love what we have in store for you on page 109. Go ahead and flip there now!

BONUS SECTION

8 Additional Chapters to Help You Increase Your Sales & Profits

Is Price Really The Issue?

"If you think a professional is expensive, wait 'til you try an amateur."
Paul "Red" Adair

Too often, far too many salespeople believe price objections kill an opportunity. Success in getting past this roadblock has less to do with product knowledge and value statements than it does with being emotionally tough enough to confront the real issues. Because so many salespeople are trained how to defend their price with discounts instead of dealing with the fear of the price objection, this age old stall tactic often stops even the most seasoned veterans right in their tracks.

One of the most common objections salespeople get is about price: "That's a bit more than we were thinking about paying." "Your prices are kind of high." "That just doesn't fit our budget." These are all typical comments. Salespeople tend to be very quick to take these comments at face value. They assume these price objections are the real issue standing between them and an order so the path of least resistance is almost always to begin dropping their price to get the sale. And, more often than not, once the price issue has been "resolved," more resistance comes to the surface.

Buyers may use the price objection as an excuse not to buy when, in fact, the real issue is different. Think about your own buying experiences. You've probably said on more than one occasion, "That's more than I wanted to spend," when what you really meant was it doesn't have the functionality you were looking for or the style just wasn't right. Or because you had no real conviction the solution would work and even under the best circumstances you probably wouldn't buy it. Sometimes price resistance is real and sometimes it's just a smoke screen. Your job is to figure it out correctly. *This is called selling.*

The first thing you must do when you hear price resistance is to make sure that it's the real issue. You want to isolate it so that you don't have to deal with any other issues later on. So, ask this question: "I don't know why this is, but typically when we hear the price is too high, it's something else in the proposal that someone didn't like, and not necessarily the price. Is that the case here?"

Now the buyer has two alternatives; they can tell you what the real issue is or they can say that everything else is fine and it's really just about price. If it's something other than price, you must deal with that. If it really is price, you should find out how far apart you are and determine whether or not you want to be responsive. Assuming you have some flexibility, ask them what would happen if you were able to reach agreement on price, or maybe what they would do if someone else paid for it. If their answer is anything other than "we'll have a deal," you need to do more qualifying or consider walking.

Isolating the objection is very important so you can deal with the real issue(s). Secondarily, when the prospect declines the opportunity to be critical of other issues in the proposal, they usually will tell you what they liked and why. When that happens, they're starting to sell themselves, and that helps you diffuse the price excuse.

Charlie Hauck & Fred Liesong

Turn Desperation Into Courage

"Once you connect with yourself, it is impossible to be lonely or desperate."
Bryant McGill

Which came first, the chicken or the egg? In sales, it's the same question asked but only with different imagery. Which came first, success or the attitude of success? Waiting to be successful instead of working with the attitude of success can be a choice that makes or breaks many salespeople.

Forget desperate housewives. What really scares buyers are desperate salespeople. How many times have you run into a sales rep who is not in sales for the love of the game, or to be the best at what they do? They act as if they need a sale to pay their bookie by Friday! Buyers have come to loathe this fast-talking, pushy pitchman stereotype.

Nobody wants to consciously be this way, but there are times when we *fail to recognize or monitor our own behavior.* Many times desperation comes because salespeople don't work on their sales plan every day. They get behind and then try to make up for lost time. A salesperson's workout is in their daily sales behavior. You have to earn your living every day. It's no different than someone working on the production floor.

In the real world, we are often under tremendous pressure to make the sale. As you allow this pressure to take hold, something changes in your approach to the buyer. You start to come across with quick answers to everything, attempt to defend every objection and push for the "Yes." Price concessions likely soon follow. You also begin to notice a change in your buyer. Your desperation shows and it has the opposite effect than the one you intended. Often, this is where the sale is lost.

Set up a mental "walk away" fund. Let's pretend for a moment that just before that last sales call you stopped at a convenience store and picked up a lottery ticket. The Million Dollar Winner! You now have enough money that you can walk away from anyone.

Now let's say you decided to stay and keep selling anyway. With the winning ticket in your pocket, do you think your attitude on that sales call would change much? Yeah, I know. You wouldn't go on the sales call. But if you did, would your attitude be different? You bet it would! Think you'd come across as desperate for the sale? Not hardly. Instead you'd be able to exude a quiet confidence that only a financially secure person would have. Your prospective buyer would notice that attitude and be more comfortable with you, and the call would probably have a better result. **Act as if** you've got that check in your pocket and watch your fortunes change.

By the way, your real life lottery ticket is a full pipeline of potential opportunities!

Do your behavior every day. Hold yourself accountable for calling on a lot of the right kind of prospects and having lots of face-to-face meetings. Emphasize decision meetings.

Miscommunication Is The Key To Failure

"A perfection of means, and confusion of aims, seems to be our main problem."
Albert Einstein

Efficient and effective communication is the backbone of success everywhere, and particularly in sales. Knowing how to recognize your own style as well as the style of others can make a significant difference in your ability to win the trust and business of your prospects. Understanding that people are the largest variable in any transaction is critical, so mastering the fundamentals of behavioral styles can give you the advantage in any business arena.

Fran just had one of those weeks where everyone he talked to seemed difficult. His inside people acted defensive, his boss had snapped his head off after a simple request, and even a few clients had blown him off after what he thought were some simple negotiations. Or so he thought.

When two people or departments are interacting, they are usually coming from the position of sharing opinions, facts, information, or emotional static. Many conversations break down when each party views the topic of conversation from a different perspective. Research tells us that when two parties have a conversation, the chance that they are both sharing information that is grounded in the same reality is less than 15%. In other words, the majority of time you are on a totally different conversation path than the other party.

Science also tells us that it is often not "what" was said, but "how" it was said that determines the direction and outcome of any conversation. For a list of "Words that Work" go to www.growdyn.com/map.

Check your tone, put your ego where it belongs and make sure to use "pillows and cushions" to set up the dialogue so that everyone is comfortable.

Which Conversation Path Are You On?

- OPINIONS: Opinions are preset ideas and attitudes. On this conversation path, you have already predetermined what to worry about and what is important. Your objectivity is tainted by your personal opinions or experience. In business, many times we need to let go of our prejudices in order to make wise decisions.

- EMOTIONAL STATIC: This conversation path ends with both parties losing perspective. Your conversation is "out of control." You see personal attacks where none are intended. Conversations are wasted on filling a personal agenda, or meeting emotional needs instead of taking care of business.

- FACTS/INFORMATION: When you are on this path your conversations are rational and logical. Your most important tool is the ability to ask questions. You take an objective position to gathering data. You do not have an opinion, nor are you emotionally involved with your own ego or personal agenda.

Get out your DISC profile and review the Dos and Don'ts of Communication while remembering that other people may have different needs or styles than yours. Learn how to "rewind" a conversation to the point where you can start over from common ground.

If you do not have a DISC profile and want to learn how to communicate better with your prospects, clients, and bosses – call us at 877-877-2920 or receive a complimentary profile at www.growdyn.com/map.

Bulldog Mentality Madness

"Sales are contingent upon the attitude of the salesman – not the attitude of the prospect."
W. Clement Stone

Bulldogs never let go once they lock on. How many salespeople can you think of that approach their marketplace with the same mentality? How many opportunities have they missed because they don't believe that there are any bad tasting catches mixed in with the good once they've locked on to a potential victim? Knowing that not everyone is a good fit allows you to understand that Bulldogs can often make good pets but very frequently they make lousy and annoying salespeople.

"Bulldog" was his nickname and he was proud of it. Chuckie spent years proving that no one could escape him once he made you a prospect. Tireless and relentless, this sales guy didn't care if it took 12 days, 12 weeks, 12 months or 12 years to get a customer. Chuckie knew he could outlast anyone as long as he could just keep stopping by and leaving his card and some literature. Sure, there were other sales people that made more than he did or spent more time living their lives, but Chuckie knew they were all the lucky ones. What did they know about working hard like "Bulldog"?

Bulldog could not dare to think that his process of never letting go was costing him opportunities or money. Persistence is often a virtue that many "sales dogs" rely on when they have not, or will not, learn new sales techniques. They believe that sooner or later all that literature and face time will pay off if they can just stick it out long enough. That attitude is not necessarily bad, as long as you don't want to earn more money and live long enough to enjoy it, though. Many seasoned sales vets bank on a positive mental attitude and a "don't take no for an answer" mentality as a primary key to success in their unending quest to close every single deal that dares to come into their field of vision. Frankly, no one has done it yet and no one ever will.

Being persistent is a great virtue in sales. *When* to be persistent is the art that few master. Chuckie left plenty of business on the street that could have been his had he been persistent *on* the call rather than *after* it. Relentless follow up should never be confused with superior selling or closing skills. Chuckie probably never figured out that had he asked one simple question, he might have saved himself hours and hours of worthless work. By asking a prospect what it takes to do business, a salesperson can decide how much effort and energy to put towards turning a suspect into a prospect and then the prospect into a customer. Chuckie figured that his showing up would prove how much he wanted the business and that the suspect would be impressed with that. Nice, wishful thinking. But not very effective.

A Rep Agency's Road MAP to Dynamic Sales Performance

Recipe For Success

"If you want to be successful, find someone who has achieved the results you want and copy what they do and you'll achieve the same results."
Tony Robbins

Success in selling, just like success in cooking, requires a recipe to produce a great final product. Approaching your market with a random collection of unrelated activities will produce no more success than a chef who just throws everything he has in a pot in an effort to make a gourmet meal.

Both Michael and his manager knew he was working hard every day, but serious questions were starting to be asked about his production. Michael was servicing his existing clients, answering and returning phone calls and emails like a champ, but there was so little progress on his top line growth that even he was starting to wonder what he was really doing with every day in the week.

It was easy enough for Michael to convince himself that he was doing his job because of all his activity, but he was confusing all the busy work for a truly productive week.

What Michael needed was a recipe for success. In Michael's case, the recipe was as simple as knowing how to practice the right sales behaviors that produce results and avoid the wrong sales behaviors that waste time. If Michael can understand what he MUST do every week, and make sense of the numbers behind that, then he can make decisions about what to do, and when to do it.

Your sales week will be much more productive if you get a sense for how to crunch these numbers:

- % Contact: If you attempted 10 phone or face-to-face approaches, how many would you actually speak with?

- % Meetings Set: If you talked to 10 prospects, how many would set a get-together with you to talk about a deal or something new?

- % Second Visits: If you had 10 first get-togethers with prospects, how many will lead to a second meeting?

- % Proposals/Presentations: If you had 10 second get-togethers with prospects, how many will lead to a proposal?

- % Sales Closed: If you had given 10 proposals or presentations, how many will lead to a sale?

- Average Sales $: If you had closed 10 sales, how much would the average sale be? (Best guess)

What is your Total Sales Target or Business Objective for the year? $_____

Now work backwards, and you will know how many first contacts, approaches or discovery meetings that you have to have every week to make your targets.

Just Get Started Already

"Would you rather tackle the first five minutes of the tough stuff, or torture yourself all day long by not doing it?"
Fred Liesong

When salespeople are in a slump, nothing seems to work, and consequently even the best will at times find themselves chained to the desk in their office. Nothing cures a slump faster and more assuredly than pure activity. Like the law of inertia says, a body at rest tends to stay at rest and a body in motion tends to stay in motion. Salespeople must remember that sales success relies as much on just getting started, making the first call, or dialing the first number as it does on closing a tough customer.

Like anyone in the business world, Ernie felt entitled to a "mental health day" after hearing excuse after excuse from prospects and existing customers. The voices in his head seemed to be amplified on those days and seemed to start playing the minute he got up. They would say that the economy is stalled, so why try; and really, who is going to take calls on a Monday, anyway? To make matters worse, his thinking would drift to thoughts like: there's no reason to make calls if I don't feel right, I'm entitled to some time off, why even start anything when I'll just get interrupted, and all the other negative internal messages we all hear from time to time. Ernie would get bogged down in his own thoughts and begin to shift his focus to the negative. But focusing on the wrong end of the process can be fatal if it isn't treated early.

One day while looking through his planner, Ernie stumbled across an old list of goals he wanted to accomplish. Provoked by the fact that nothing on his list was "checked off," Ernie made a deal with himself to **commit to just fifteen minutes of calls**, no matter what happened, good or bad.

With his goal list in hand, Ernie sat down and picked up the phone. By the time he looked up, three hours had passed, thirty calls were made, several opportunities were uncovered, and Ernie didn't even realize he had missed lunch.

Ernie's list of goals really helped snap him out of the funk he was in that day. Without them he would have no reason to get going at all. Once he recommitted to accomplishing the things on that list, **all he had to do was start.**

Worrying about finishing a task or about the outcome when you are struggling with the messages that justify doing nothing has killed countless careers before they even got started. Ernie reasoned that finishing anything, let alone getting a win, was impossible without getting started somewhere. By making a game out of surviving the first few minutes, the task was reduced to a manageable size that almost guaranteed getting the good vibes going again.

When you want to accomplish anything, do the hardest part first and the rest seems to fall in line once your momentum builds. Turn down the volume on the blues and pick up the phone or set a meeting. Can you give *yourself* the same chance to experience the success that Ernie did on a day that looked doomed from the outset?

Get Out Of The Mind Reading Business

"The fruit of empty hopes is more bitter than the saddest truth."
Angel Wagenstein

Everyone knows the old joke about the problem with the word ASSUME: it makes an *#& out of you and me! The last thing you want to do on a sales call is assume what a prospect or customer is thinking. Taking the time to ask enough of the right questions is always more efficient and effective than fixing a problem that should've never occurred.

Ever witness a business meeting where there seemed to be little structure, where both parties seemed to be on different pages, where expectations were not met, and little was accomplished? Even worse, you expected something positive to occur, but simply got a lukewarm response such as, "I need to think it over. Call me in a few days." Opportunities are squandered and the buyer seems to be in control.

All too often sales calls are "professional visits." Many visits are unstructured; objectives are not determined or communicated. **Premature presentations are usually the result.** During the show up and throw up phase, an abundance of mind reading seems to take place. Assumptions are made that the buyer knows why you are there, why your latest and greatest offering is a no-brainer and no clarification of purpose is needed. Most salespeople are poor mind readers.

The key to successfully taking the lead in the selling interview is to establish a "process expectation" early in the meeting. You must first determine with your prospect the amount of time available for the meeting and what they would like to accomplish for it to be successful. Next, obtain permission to ask questions to get a better understanding of the prospect's issues and priorities, and agree that at the end of the meeting, at the very least, you'll make a decision as to whether or not to continue talking.

If you have a very clear meeting agreement, you'll build tremendous rapport with the prospect, improve communication significantly because both parties have the opportunity to ask questions, eliminate premature presentations, get decisions, and eliminate "think it overs." In addition, our clients tell us that prospects visibly begin to relax when they hear that the seller is comfortable with hearing "No." The meeting agreement is one of the most effective selling tools you'll ever own. Master it and you're well on your way to becoming a true sales superstar.

Are You Pushing Or Pulling?

"Opportunities are usually disguised as hard work, so most people don't recognize them."
Ann Landers

Are you getting paid to take all the pressure in a sales or decision meeting or would you rather share that mutually with the buyer? What would happen if you chose a process that would let a prospective buyer do their fair share of the work to get to a Yes or No decision? Very few people like to be sold, but almost everybody likes to make a decision they are comfortable with and were allowed to make for their own reasons. Give them the opportunity to do both and learn to enjoy the process and the profession of sales.

Unskilled salespeople are so predictable! They use the "pull" approach, constantly trying to convince and persuade the buyer to buy from them. Of course, the buyers are on to these tactics and are doing their best to "push" the salesperson away. Often, even buyers who are ready to buy will feel trapped and push the salesperson away because they don't want to be sold.

Clearly, a new approach is needed. Why not give the buyer a little room to operate? Giving the buyer an option to exit can have magical results when you have a sincere buyer. This gives you a chance to probe for problems and priorities and get "in the ways" out of the way, or go for a "No," thus arriving at the right conclusion for both parties without wasting everyone's time. In any case, rapport is maintained, even strengthened, and you're doing the disqualifying, not them.

An "easy exit" is an opportunity for you to make the buyer feel comfortable by bringing up situations that may still be a source of concern. Unless you want to take all the pressure on yourself, the old fashioned way, it's better to let the buyer make decisions about their own problems. In effect, you're providing them with an "easy exit." You'll find that one of two things will happen: 1) they'll convince you that your concern is unwarranted and that it's really not an issue (proving to you that they really are sincere) or 2) they'll admit that your concern is valid. Here are some examples:

- "If we don't have a fit, it's okay to tell me."

- "We may invest some time together today looking at your situation only to find that we're not the right solution for you. If we're not, you need to be comfortable telling me that. Okay?"

- "That problem doesn't sound like it's causing you that much trouble. Are you sure it's really important enough to do something about it?"

- "Would it be fair to say that it sounds like the company isn't really that committed to finding a solution just yet?"

- "I get the feeling that this is much more than you had planned to invest. Do we need to talk about that some more?"

It helps to keep your "antenna" up at all times to assess what the buyer is implying when they make a statement. Often a buyer will not tell you the whole truth regarding a problem, but will send out bits of (mis)information instead. It's your job to relieve pressure and help discover what the buyer is really saying.

Your role is to gently diminish and deny their problems and priorities and their commitment to do something to fix it, thus getting them to defend their position and prove to you that they are ready to take action. In essence, you are actually giving them a gentle but nurturing push. Any time you give them a chance to run away from doing business with you and they don't take it, they're sending a message that they want to do business!

About Charlie Hauck

Drawing on more than 25 years of experience working with leaders focused on both personal and professional growth, Charlie shares his experience, creativity and savvy in understanding his clients' particular challenges. By respecting the differences in the wide variety of businesses and industries his clients represent, Charlie believes it is the people, rather than any of their technologies, that create the most lasting successes. By making that the foundation of all his work with both individuals and teams, Charlie's clients have been successful in all types of industries and organizations, ranging from healthcare providers, manufacturing, distribution, non-profits, and a diverse group of companies at all levels of the business world.

Past and current clients include both regional and national companies and organizations in the professional services, distribution, manufacturing, and technology arenas. Growth Dynamics also has a wide range of experience in the utilization of instruments, assessments, and processes to support hiring, selection, and development of individuals and teams that make up successful and growing organizations.

Charlie and the Growth Dynamics team have become heavily committed to bringing their processes and experience to many different markets where the primary focus on human interaction is immensely important to growth and success.

Charlie's pastime activities include hanging out with his grandchildren, traveling to the shore, skiing out west (four knee surgeries later) and riding one of his many bicycles.

About Fred Liesong

Fred joined Growth Dynamics as an associate in 2003 and became Operating Partner of the LLC (with Charlie Hauck) in 2006. He contributes the practical knowledge gained from over 25 years of sales, sales management, and operations experience in healthcare, technology, and consulting.

A continuous and successful history of opening new territories, introducing new products, and founding his own start-up company has provided him with a broad perspective on the challenges of creating, growing, and retaining a solid business base. Having worked with both large corporations and smaller startup firms, Fred has acquired the skills and working knowledge needed to manage a wide variety of business issues in direct sales, channel marketing and strategic partnerships.

As a sales professional, he has studied and employed many different sales and management strategies, leading to numerous performance awards throughout his career. An ability to implement any part of a growth strategy is the result of his experience in operations, mentoring sales teams, working with complex sales cycles and analyzing opportunities in the marketplace. He is a proponent of developing repeatable internal processes that allow all team members to easily execute critical business activities with maximum impact.

Significant entrepreneurial experience came as the owner of Ultimate Software in Philadelphia, where he co-founded a VAR business focused on the highly competitive market of Human Resource and Payroll Information Systems, which eventually led to an IPO. During this time, he gained valuable insights on how synergistic team cooperation, shared common goals, and creativity can propel even the smallest companies to success.

Based on a unique sense of implementation, strategy and tactics, Fred can help to overcome the frustrations and hidden obstacles of consistently growing the top and bottom lines.

When he's not working, Fred enjoys trading equity options, riding his bicycle on the nearby Montour Trail, or fishing in his Bass Tracker on the local lakes and rivers.

About Growth Dynamics

Growth Dynamics provides non-traditional, counter-intuitive sales, sales management, and sales training to a wide variety of businesses, including manufacturers, distributors, contractors, and manufacturers' rep agencies. Growth Dynamics focuses on helping people rethink many of the concepts they currently use in the business development process, with emphasis on the interactions that occur in human to human dialogs.

Past and current clients include both regional and national companies such as Pepco Sales & Marketing, Northeastern Supply, Manufacturers Marketing Inc., Brandon Associates, Hufcor Inc., Preferred Sales Inc, Nexus Sales, Mullen Corp., The Granite Group, PAMS Inc., The Duff Company, Smith and Stevenson, Mid-City Supply, Rich-Tomkins, and Felker Brothers.

Charlie Hauck & Fred Liesong

Hire Growth Dynamics To Speak

Growth Dynamics has been helping teams of all sorts develop the skills and mental awareness to become High Performers for over 20 years. Our topics are aimed at helping you conquer the obstacles that typically appear as "Hidden Agents" lurking below the surface ... difficult to identify and consequently hard to fix. With a unique sense of diagnostic ability aided by our deep assessment toolset, we can present topics specific to a group or team.

Charlie Hauck, Lead Coach and Speaker, can present a variety of topics at your conference or meeting. Below are some Sales-specific presentations to choose from:

Ten Keys to Over Achieving: Business owners and managers want to believe their sales teams have that *do whatever it takes* attitude, and most sales people claim they do. The real challenge is helping your team know what the real key ingredients to over achievement really are.

Upgrading MBA (My Business Acumen): With customers wanting to know how your product or service can actually benefit them, sales people today must learn how to discuss the real business impact they can provide to their clients. Features and Benefits are not enough to get the sale; knowing how you can provide profit or reduce cost to a business owner is where the deal can be closed.

Person vs. Performance: The real magic dust for sales growth and success is not another tactic or tracking mechanism. The people who can truly separate what they do from who they are will make the greatest strides. This is a back to basics program focused on this one key ingredient that people learn and forget before internalizing its power. This concept might just be the one thing that makes or breaks many sales careers.

Selling to NO Is Not a Trick: So many salespeople feel relief when they first hear that getting to "No" is allowed. That just might be where the problem starts for many, though. The power of "No" in the sales process must be carried through to an actual conclusion of the pursuit, yet many salespeople that have learned this technique use it as a launching pad to revert back to the same old stuff.

Business Planning for Your Team: Too many salespeople do not have a plan for their market and territories. This program defines business planning on a personal level and discusses factors that stop people from creating a real business plan.

Other Sales-specific topics:

- Time Management
- Goal Setting and Problem Solving
- Precise Communication
- Motivational Success System
- Accountability
- Concept of Money

- Emotional Discipline
- Need for Approval
- Supportive Beliefs
- Account Development Strategies
- Territory Management
- Qualifying

Contact us to have a conversation so we can help you choose which topic is right for you and your organization: info@growthdynamicsonline.com | 877-877-2930

Or see more details at www.growdyn.com/speak.

FREE Sales Performance Webcast

Are you seeing your fair share of opportunities, but not able to capitalize on enough of them?

Are you sick and tired of babysitting inconsistent salespeople?

Are you frustrated with trying to understand why some reps are so successful and others are not?

If you answered YES to any of these questions, then we may have some <u>actionable</u> and revealing answers for you! Because for a limited time, we're offering FREE Sales Performance Webcasts to readers of our book.

Typically we charge anywhere between $1,000-$2,000 for these webcasts. But...for the readers of our book...we're gifting you and your team a Sales Performance Webcast that you will never forget!

Please understand, though, that we cannot help everybody. Our methods may or may not be right for your company. For that reason, to qualify, **you must give us a call or send an email – and ask about this special, one-time offer.**

After an initial consult conversation about your company and your goals, if we both agree that we're the right fit for you and your sales philosophy, we'll book a time to deliver a CUSTOM Sales Performance Webcast that will help your team remove mental road blocks, perform at a higher standard, and increase revenues!

That's right...if we're the right fit we'll create a custom webcast that's specific for YOUR company and YOUR needs – based on our initial consult conversation!

In addition, after the webcast, we will provide a **30-day free subscription to our weekly Monday Morning Manager for ALL participants** (*a $250 annual value per subscriber*) – **AND** – 60 minutes of post-meeting coaching support for management (*a $250 value*).

As you can see, you have nothing to lose and everything to gain – call us today at 877-877-2920 or send a note to info@growthdynamicsonline.com or go to www.growdyn.com/mapcast.

www.ingramcontent.com/pod-product-compliance
Lightning Source LLC
Chambersburg PA
CBHW071721170526
45165CB00005B/2098